essentials

After Dinner Speaking

Time-saving books that teach specific skills to busy people, focusing on what really matters: the things that make a difference – the *essentials*. Other books in the series include:

Speak Out with Confidence
Entertain with Confidence
Toasts and Short Speeches
Speaking in Public
Making the Bride's Father's Speech
Making the Bridegroom's Speech
Making the Best Man's Speech
Making Great Presentations
Writing Good Reports
Responding to Stress
Succeeding at Interviews
Solving Problems
Hiring People
Getting Started on the Internet
Feeling Good for No Good Reason

For full details please send for a free copy of the latest catalogue. See back cover for address.

The things that really matter about

After Dinner Speaking

Second Edition

John Bowden

ESSENTIALS

First published in 2000 by
How To Books Ltd, 3 Newtec Place,
Magdalen Road, Oxford OX4 1RE, United Kingdom
Tel: (01865) 793806   Fax: (01865) 248780
email: info@howtobooks.co.uk
www.howtobooks.co.uk

First edition published 2000
Second edition 2000

British Library Cataloguing in Publication Data.
A catalogue record for this book is available from
the British Library.

Edited by Diana Brueton
Cover design by Shireen Nathoo Design
Produced for How To Books by Deer Park Productions
Typeset by Anneset, Weston-super-Mare, Somerset
Printed and bound in Great Britain

ESSENTIALS *is an imprint of*
How To Books

Contents

Preface

The audience is well wined and amply dined. It is the traditional time for brandy, cigars and laughter. This should be an orator's dream, yet all too often it turns into a nightmare as speakers who have been too apprehensive to enjoy the food, instead make a meal of the speech. Don't allow this to happen to you.

An after dinner speech should be light-hearted, humorous and friendly. It should not deal with 'big' issues. People want to get away from all the serious stuff that dominates their everyday lives and just have a good laugh. The trick is to construct a tailor-made script that packs a punch and has real impact yet has the appearance of being nothing more than a laid back, spontaneous and entertaining chat with friends.

Heard the one about the writer who used masculine nouns and pronouns throughout his book? This stems from my desire to avoid ugly, cumbersome English. No discrimination, prejudice or bias is intended. This book really is written for *everyone* who wants to make speeches which are relevant, topical, fast, punchy, funny – and downright impressive. Women and men should have an equal right to buy it!

John Bowden

1 Learning the Essentials

After dinner speaking isn't a natural activity.
It's like golf – no one can play well first time. It's a
learnt skill.

(Bob Monkhouse)

4 *things that really matter*

1 **MAKING IT ENTERTAINING**

2 **KNOWING YOUR AUDIENCE**

3 **DEVELOPING YOUR THEME**

4 **CONFIRMING THE PROGRAMME**

After dinner audiences want to be entertained. For that reason you should avoid the touchingly sentimental, thoughtful and profound and instead concentrate on the frivolous, off-beat and amusing.

If you're going to appear before an unfamiliar bunch of faces, research is vital. Take the time to find out who they are, what they want to hear and what they are capable of grasping quickly and easily. If your most subtle joke misfires because the audience doesn't get it, it's really not their fault, it's yours.

Try not to leave it too long before you speak. A mellow, relaxed audience will laugh at even your weakest jokes and will forgive you a multitude of sins. A drunken crowd can turn on you like a dyspeptic rottweiler.

IS THIS YOU?

● *This will be the first time I've spoken after dinner . . . except during other people's speeches. Help!* ● *I've been disappointed with my previous efforts at after dinner speaking and want to improve.* ● *I need to make a one-off after dinner speech. I'm a specialist in my field, but an inexperienced public speaker.* ● *I've been making after dinner speeches for years. I am quite confident but feel it's time to add a little polish to my act.* ● *With some audiences my speeches seem to go down well, with others they just go down. Don't ask me why.*

① MAKING IT ENTERTAINING

The basic purpose of an after dinner speech is to entertain. While the occasional injection of a serious note can sometimes serve as a much-needed anchor, the seriousness should never be allowed to predominate. You want your speech to come over as a light and amusing social chat with friends.

Your overall aim is to leave your audience feeling happier during and after your speech than they were before it.

An after dinner speech should be:

● **Optimistic**. This is not the time to share your personal woes, paint a gloomy picture of the present or offer dire predictions about the future. Leave your soapbox at home. You are not here to instruct or persuade. Keep the overall tone light and upbeat. Give them what they want to hear and what the occasion requires.

● **Uncomplicated**. Don't make your audience strain to get your point. Develop your speech around a central theme and one or two simple, straightforward points that they can easily grasp.

- **Enlivened with humour.** You need to use humour as a tool throughout your speech. Include plenty of little quips, one-liners and funny stories. But make sure all your humorous remarks are entirely in character with the audience, with the occasion and with you.

Your humour must always be appropriate. Appropriateness is the key to effectiveness.

② KNOWING YOUR AUDIENCE

As a speaker, you have to acknowledge the importance of your audience and include them. You really have no choice. If you ignore them, they won't be entertained. If they're not entertained, your speech will have failed. A speaker *needs* the attention of his audience. They *have* to listen, and their laughter *has* to be spontaneous, otherwise it's worthless.

Each passage of your speech should produce the right kind of buzz in at least one key element of the audience. If it doesn't it's a waste of words.

A prospector does not go out and simply start drilling holes randomly in the hope that one of them will hit the spot. No, he knows the earth will be the source of his eventual wealth, but first he must do his groundwork. He must discover where oil is likely to be found, and only then will he drill to produce that gusher. In the same way, a speaker must regard his audience as the source that will supply *his* reward. But first he must study them to find out where most mirth is likely to be mined.

The key to good after dinner speaking is to 'think audience'. Always remember that there is only one ultimate judge of the effectiveness of a speech and that is the audience. The audience is supreme.

Revellers at a stag party won't be entertained by the same material as a matinee of senior citizens. Teenagers go for zany, madcap jokes. Old folks prefer slower, broad anecdotal humour. Audiences in their twenties appreciate speed, wit and sophistication. Thirty-, forty- and fifty-somethings prefer a little 'adult humour'.

Generalisations? Of course. But teenagers won't laugh at the same material as their parents. Each generation has a different outlook and sense of humour. Don't just play to your own age.

Know more about your audience than you need to know. The more information you have in reserve, the more selective you can be about what you choose to say and how you choose to say it. It's far easier to cut bad material than to put new material in. *Write long and then cut hard and relentlessly.* Your speech will be greatly enhanced if you trust in the Principle of the Survival of the Fittest.

Understanding what people want to hear means *listening more than speaking.* An architect cannot build you a house unless he knows how you want to live. Your hairdresser cannot give you a good haircut unless you have told him how you want to look when he's finished. You cannot tell people what they want to hear, unless you have found out first.

To win an audience's allegiance, you must first meet its expectations. To fail to win its allegiance is the kiss of death.

DEVELOPING YOUR THEME

A speech without a theme is like a car without an engine: the only way it can go is downhill.

You must have a proposition, a single dominant idea running throughout.

Choose a clear, central theme that suits the occasion and audience. Go for one that's novel, provocative and original – but don't overdo it – you want to entertain, not shock.

Slant your theme to suit your audience. You need to find one which this particular audience will identify with and find relevant and interesting. It must be general enough to fit the allotted time, but specific enough to be meaningful to your audience.

Too wide	Just right	Too narrow
Golf	The forthcoming season	Nick's hole-in-one
XYZ Ltd	A review of the year	The reorganisation of accounts
I.T.	A parody of conference buzzwords	My new ThinkPad

All your intimate confessions, witty observations, perceptive one-liners, amusing anecdotes and hilarious insights into the state of the world must then be appropriate to this core theme.

 CONFIRMING THE PROGRAMME

You should know well in advance when and for how long you will be expected to speak. The usual order of speeches at a formal do is as follows:

- **The Loyal Toast**. The toastmaster proposes the toast to Her Majesty the Queen. This may be followed by the simultaneous ignition of matches and lighters accompanied by an evening chorus of spluttering and coughs.

- **The toast to the host organisation**. If the occasion involves a company, corporation, society or club, someone will talk about its history and discuss an issue of current interest to the audience.

- **The response**. The chairperson makes his contribution to the evening.

- **The toast to the guests**. One of your hosts names the top table guests, saving you, as principal speaker, for last.

Make sure someone introduces you. Never introduce yourself, even if you are well known to every person in the room.

And don't leave the wording of the announcement to chance. Write a short, crisp introduction and hand it to the MC to read out. Firmly yet politely make it abundantly clear that the audience should *not* be told that you provided your own intro. Otherwise he is likely to use the fact to get a cheap laugh – and at *your* expense.

Your introduction should set the right tone for your speech. Here are a few possibilities:

'It isn't often that I have the pleasure of introducing a truly great after dinner speaker – and tonight is no exception. Please welcome . . .'

'I'm not going to stand around and bore you with a lot of pathetic old jokes. Instead, I'm going to introduce a man who can do that much better than I can . . .'

'A man like our guest speaker is certainly hard to find. Tonight, for instance, we had to look in three pubs and a wine bar. But we found him. Please put your hands together to welcome . . .'

- **Your response**. It's showtime! Don't forget to include a few words of thanks to the hosts on behalf of yourself and the other guests.

- **Vote of thanks**. Finally, the chairperson will probably rise to give a short vote of thanks to round off the evening.

MAKING WHAT MATTERS WORK FOR YOU

✓ Make happy talk

✓ To fail to prepare is to prepare to fail. You *must* find out what your audience wants to hear. Only then can you begin to think about what you are going to say and how you are going to say it.

✓ Base your speech around one core theme that's meaningful to *this* audience and find out precisely where you fit into the evening's programme of toasts and responses.

✓ Find out who is to introduce you and agree with them the precise form of words to be used.

2 Choosing the Right Material

The ideal after dinner speech is no more than 12 minutes long and a successful one involves keeping the audience laughing for at least eight minutes.

(Sir John Harvey-Jones)

4

things that
really matter

1 **KEEPING IT RELEVANT**

2 **INVENTING JOKES**

3 **SWITCHING JOKES**

4 **GETTING THE TONE RIGHT**

A good after dinner speech includes an entertaining balance of humorous one-liners, longer stories and friendly mickey-taking – all possibly underpinned by one or two more serious thoughts.

The material you choose must be right for *this* audience, for *this* occasion – and for *you*. A firm's annual dinner will give you the chance to make a few humorous remarks about a rival's lousy products; at a football club dance you could kick-off with some soccer stories.

From the moment you begin to speak the audience is asking itself: 'Is this speech for me?' This gives you a wonderful opportunity to get in quickly with the right answer. Within 30 seconds the audience should be telling itself: 'Yes, this speech *is* for me! It's relevant, original, topical . . . What's more, it's fun!'

IS THIS YOU?

● *I am going to make a speech at my company's annual dinner, but I'm not sure what sort of thing to say.* ● *Some of my jokes are ancient. Does it matter?* ● *None of the audience has met me. Should this affect my choice of material?* ● *I've heard it said that it's a good idea to refer to some current news event. What's the point?* ● *I don't want my speech to be 'squeaky clean', but I don't know how far I should go.*

① KEEPING IT RELEVANT

To be interesting, entertaining and memorable *your material needs to be meaningful* to the audience. They must *identify* with your words and sentiments.

The vital thing with a tight-knit group is to establish yourself immediately as an insider, to make references only they will understand, so that right from your first few sentences they feel that you are one of them – whether you are or not.

An audience will always enjoy a speech more if they are made a part of it. Here are a few ways to convince people that you have a real understanding of their specialised world.

● **Tell them what they want to hear.** Think audience and think theme. There's nothing wrong with preaching to the converted. Audiences *like* to be told things they already know and they *love* to hear opinions with which they concur.

If you want to ingratiate yourself with an audience – and you should want to – use *your* humour to reinforce *their* views. If they believe strongly in green issues, then you might remark: 'If you want to take a bath in this city, the water leaves a ring around *you*.'

- **Tell meaningful stories**. Everyone loves a story. If you can find a relevant anecdote or gag you are onto a winner. Matching your choice of anecdotes and jokes to the nature of the audience is easy when the group is homogeneous – medical stories for doctors, religious anecdotes for the clergy, horsey tales for the gymkhana club.

  If you are addressing an audience of fishermen in Scotland, they will not warm to a story set in a gay disco in San Francisco. Yet if you are speaking to an audience of amateur cricketers, a blow by blow account of a number 11 batsman's final over heroics is sure to bowl them over.

- **Know their history**. A few references to the history of this illustrious company, club or society are sure to go down well. However, make sure you get your facts right. *Cave anorakem* (beware of the anorak).

- **Use your local knowledge**. What are the locals currently complaining about? Maybe the traffic wardens are being a little over-zealous in the city centre. Perhaps the Mormons have just hit town. Whatever the perceived problem, reverse it, and consider including it as a 'funny thing happened to me' line.

  'A funny thing happened to me on the way here this evening:

  – the traffic lights were working in Queen's Square.

  – I didn't see a fight outside the King's Head.

  – my train was on time.'

- **Exploit their irritations**. Every organisation has one current overriding collective gripe. Exploit it.

  'The trouble with (*their current Mr Nasty*) is that he is suffering from paralysis of the intellect.'

  '(*Mr Nasty*) is the kind of man who would cut down a 200-year-old oak and mount the stump to make a speech on conservation.'

  'I hear they're erecting a huge statue of (*Mr Nasty*) in Trafalgar Square. They are doing it so the pigeons can express the views of all of us.'

- **Focus on shared experiences**. Talk about experiences that you shared with the audience. Relate anecdotes that help the audience tap into common events.

  'Didn't we have a blooming good time on our visit to the Chelsea Flower Show . . . ?'

- **Foster group spirit**. Your aim should be to create social cohesion and good feelings. Make your audience feel proud to work for *this* company, to be involved in this sales launch, to be a member of *this* golf club. Remind them of the values and experiences they share. Concentrate on whatever it is that binds them together.

- **Make it original**. There's an awful lot of people out there who have had funny or strange experiences. Has something quirky ever happened to you? If you have a story or convincing tale to tell, then why not spin the yarn at your club or company dinner? Audiences want to hear something *different, unusual and interesting.* Most of all, they want to be *entertained.*

- **Use whatever works for you.** Paradoxically, if you pinch material from one person, it's called plagiarism. If you steal it from 20, it's called research. There's a moral there somewhere. The following anecdote was heard recently at a football club's end-of-season dinner:

  'Kevin's a generous manager. He took the whole team out for an end-of-season meal. The boss told the waiter that he'd have steak and kidney pie. "And the vegetables?" the waiter asked. "Oh, they'll have the same," Kevin said.'

  This leaders-and-led story went down well – not least amongst the vegetables. No one seemed to recall a very similar tale being told about Margaret Thatcher and her Cabinet in the mid-1980s. The speaker had found an almost perfect fit and made a few minor adjustments. You can do the same. Just try to look through potential source material with a fresh eye.

  If you find a story about Florence Nightingale that could help expound your theme, make a few embellishments here and there and allow your society treasurer to play the role of the Lady of the Lamp. If you find an ideal line by Mark Twain, put it in the mouth of your company chairman.

Don't allow the facts to spoil a good story. As Woody Allen didn't say, 'Your aim is to be entertaining, not necessarily accurate.'

- **Be topical.** You win Brownie points for topicality. A story based on – or even just referring to – *a current event, news item* or *piece of local gossip* will tell them this speech was written specifically for them, because an identical one could not possibly have been delivered before.

What an audience knows is a dynamic thing. It's constantly changing. New information becomes available, and old information becomes tired and fades away. Today's hot topic is tomorrow's yesterday's news.

How can you know your audience's current knowledge of events? A few enquiries may help, but it often comes down to a gut feeling and to common sense. A big story that broke yesterday or even a few hours ago is safe, a lesser story that broke within the last hour isn't.

 INVENTING JOKES

Every joke you hear has been 'built' by someone. And that person had exactly the same materials as you have now. Let's see how you can use those raw materials to create *customised comedy*.

> 'Our local vet and taxidermist have merged with the slogan: "Either way you get your dog back"'.

Why is this funny? Because of its construction. Set-up . . . sting. Rephrase the same idea and it falls apart. If the line had been:

> 'You are sure to get your dog back now whatever the outcome of the operation because our local vet and taxidermist have joined forces'

the comedy is lost. The joke is too cumbersome and the set-up and tagline have been reversed.

A good way to kick-start your comic creativity is to *begin* with the punchline and then *work back* to create the set-up!

Let me explain. Say you want to devise a few jokes on the theme of crime and punishment. You begin by thinking about cops and robbers. What do they do? Cops look for *leads, nick* people and ask them to *accompany* them to the station. Robbers get *charged, let off* or *put away*. Then ask yourself whether any of these key words you have come up with have any other meanings which could serve as joke set-ups. Dogs have leads; razor blades nick you; singers are accompanied by pianos. So you might come up with the following:

> 'A man broke into Battersea Dogs Home and stole all the animals. None of the dogs have been recovered but the police say they've got plenty of leads.'

> 'A burglar broke into a razor factory . . . he got nicked.'

> 'A man was caught breaking into a piano factory . . . he was asked to accompany the police to the station.'

> 'A man broke into a power station while his mate broke into a fireworks factory. The first man got charged, the second got let off.'

> 'A thief broke into a storage container factory . . . he got put away.'

Types of jokes

Most gags come under one – or occasionally more than one – of the following categories. Let's take the theme of doctors and nurses to illustrate them. The techniques employed in fashioning each form of frivolity are usually self-evident, although a few words of explanation have been added, where necessary:

- **Exaggeration**. He's never had a day's sickness in his life. He always makes it last at least three months.

- **The insult**. She's a lousy nurse. She couldn't even put a dressing on a salad.

- **Illogical logic**. I went to the doctor's this morning. I couldn't go last week – I was sick.

- **The pun**. A paediatrician is a man with little patients.

- **Word play** (not to be confused with puns). I told my doctor that my irregular heartbeat was bothering me. He said, 'Don't worry. We'll soon put a stop to it.'

- **The picture** (the gag creates a mental picture). No nurse, I said prick his boil!

- **The reverse**. A man walks into a doctor's surgery with a duck on his head. The doctor says, 'What can I do for you?' And the duck replies, 'I want this wart on my foot removed.'

- **The twisted cliché**. An apple a day keeps the doctor away . . . and so does living in the wrong postal code area.

- **Truthfulness**. A specialist is a doctor with a smaller practice but a bigger home.

③ SWITCHING JOKES

So far we've stressed the importance of choosing the right sort of material for your speech and discussed ways you can devise your own jokes. Now let's talk about *switching* gags. What you have to do is take the *idea* behind a funny but as yet unrelated gag and then transfer it to the subject and theme of your speech.

Say you need some golfing gags. Here are a few examples

of how jokes on a variety of topics can be switched to meet your needs.

1. 'When we were in the National Gallery, I overheard this elderly man ask his wife what she thought of the Picasso exhibition. "It's not bad," she said, "but I prefer art." '

Switch: 'I once played 18 holes with Nick Faldo at St Andrews. As the round ended, I asked timidly, "What do you think of my game?" And Faldo said, "Not bad, but I still prefer golf." '

2. 'When I asked Dave why he was so relaxed about his overdraft, he said, "Because it's grown big enough to look after itself." '

Switch: 'I'm not in the *least* worried about my handicap. Believe me, it's big enough to look after itself.'

3. 'This old lady down the Post Office asked me how to do the National Lottery. It was a double rollover Saturday and she'd decided to have a flutter for the first time. So I showed her. "But how do you know *which* six numbers will win?" she asked.'

Switch: 'Then there was this sweet young thing who was being initiated into the mysteries of the glorious game by her boyfriend. "And tell me," she said coyly, "which club do I use to make a hole-in-one?" '

4. 'An ancient philosopher once told his young pupil, "Together, we shall explore the meaning of life and unravel the mysteries of the universe." The pupil looked up at his mentor and said, "Great . . . and what are we going to do tomorrow?" '

Switch: 'Two women approached (club professional) in the club shop. "Do you wish to learn to play golf, madam?" he asked one. "Oh no," she said, "it's my friend who wants to learn. I learnt yesterday." '

5. 'Bart began to enter the details required on the front of his examination paper. But he couldn't remember the number of the exam centre, and he didn't know the centre's reference number, the exam code, or even the date. In frustration, he turned to his neighbour and exclaimed, "This is a difficult exam, isn't it?" '

Switch: 'A guest on (*local*) golf course placed the ball in position, swung and missed it three times, hit it the fourth time, and then turned to his host and said, "This is a difficult course, isn't it?" '

④ GETTING THE TONE RIGHT

What is acceptable and what isn't in the context of a speech depends on so many factors that it would be foolish to attempt to lay down any hard and fast rules. The venue, the age and composition of the audience, even the time of day – all of these must be taken into consideration.

Indelicate language at an afternoon charity affair in the village hall could easily create the speech from hell; a routine at a rugby club stag night would be disastrous if it were not as blue as the Danube.

When it comes to questions of taste and taboos, propriety and political correctness, things continually change. You have to keep up with the changes. You must *use your own judgement and common sense* about the question and perhaps *take advice from the dinner's organiser.*

Before you tell a story or crack a joke *ask yourself* whether it passes this four-part test which Bob Monkhouse devised for all his potential material:

- Do *I* think this is funny?

- Can I say it confidently?

- Is there any danger of offending anyone?

- Will they understand and appreciate it?

If you have any doubts about your material, cut it. It may be a stunningly good wheeze in your opinion, but if you offend or embarrass your audience, you will have a very hard time winning them over again. Follow this showbiz adage: *If in doubt, leave it out.*

MAKING WHAT MATTERS WORK FOR YOU

✓ **Think audience. If people can see how what you're telling them applies to their own lives, they remain interested.**

✓ **Devise, switch or borrow whatever material works for you. Everything 'new' is derivative to a certain extent. Paradoxically, if you can find, adapt and personalise some 'old' material to make it relevant and meaningful to an audience, you are being highly creative and original.**

✓ **Throw in a couple of topical references to show them you're on the ball.**

✓ **Fashions change, and what is the accepted norm today would have been unthinkable a few years ago. So keep your finger on the pulse and don't be afraid to seek advice and guidance from the organiser of the event. You *must* get the tone right.**

3 Targeting Humour and Compliments at Individuals

If you don't know them already, find out about key personalities in the audience. You'll feel more bonded to them; they'll appreciate your efforts; and everyone will experience a more personal occasion.   (Rachael Heyhoe Flint)

3

things that really matter

1 **TAKING A FEW FRIENDLY POT SHOTS**

2 **SUGARING YOUR TEASING REMARKS WITH PRAISE**

3 **DEALING WITH HECKLERS**

The contents of this chapter come with a health – and possibly wealth – warning: *know your audience.* Sometimes even the friendliest little digs at individuals present, even when made in the best possible taste, are totally unacceptable in an after dinner speech. But this is very rare; audiences generally expect to hear them – and 'victims' usually love to receive them. Only you know the nature of the occasion and the attitude of any bigwigs likely to be present. If you don't, find out! If insults are out, fast forward to page 33.

Now that disclaimer is out of the way, we can begin to have some fun. If your speech is to the members of a sports or social club, friendly jibes and a little banter are par for the course. In a corporate context you must be a little more wary.

IS THIS YOU?

● I want to take the mickey out of my hosts. But how far should I go? ● My boss is a good sport and I'm sure he'll accept a little public humiliation in the right spirit! ● How can I be sure that my 'victims' won't be offended? ● Of course I want to be congratulatory and upbeat, but I want to do it in a way that doesn't make me sound like a complete wally. ● I'm expecting a little ribbing from one or two people in the audience. It would be useful to have a few lines prepared which I could throw back at them, if this happens.

(1) TAKING A FEW FRIENDLY POT SHOTS

At most dinners, a little friendly ribbing is called for. If properly done, it shows the audience you've done your homework, it shifts attention away from you and onto them, and it bonds and reinforces group spirit.

Choose your victims with care; some people love being the centre of attention while others hate it. Ultimately, it's a question of personality – both theirs and yours.

To start your little grey cells working on this, here are three targets that are *usually* fair game and three others that should *usually* be treated as protected species.

Most audiences will feel perfectly comfortable if you target your humour at: *yourself, local characters, your competitors or rivals.*

● **Yourself**. Mirror, mirror on the wall who's the fairest target of them all? Before you have a go at anyone else, you must first mock yourself. Let them see you're a good sport. Show them you don't take yourself too seriously:

'I'm such an unlucky guy . . . if I were reincarnated I'd probably come back as myself.'

Self-mockery of this kind is a subtle demonstration of your underlying self-confidence (honestly!). It offends nobody. More importantly though, it grants you licence to take a pop at others. If you are seen to be able to take it, it follows that you will be allowed to dish it out – and that's when the real fun starts.

- **Local characters**. Every club, society and business has one or two larger-than-life characters. Bring them into your speech. But remember that your audience will only laugh at a parody of what it *recognises* as their little foibles. Ask yourself: *Why* are they considered to be characters? Is it something to do with the way they dress, their mannerisms, or perhaps their unusual jobs or strange hobbies?

The guests must recognise that while all your jokes are clearly exaggerations, they are nonetheless based on fundamental truths about your 'victims'. For instance, there is no point in laughing at a character's colourful use of language, unless you are sure the audience knows he spends most of his waking hours effing and blinding, and is not merely the kind who just might bleat out an apologetic 'oh, blast' – and then only if mauled by a lion.

If it's well known that he's a high-flying legal eagle who's always swift to rook his clients, you could say:

'I dreamt that (*character*) died and went to the gates of heaven where he was interviewed by St Peter to see if he should be let into heaven or hell. "I don't know why I died so young," complained (*character*), "it doesn't seem fair, I'm only (*age*)." "I know," replied St Peter, "But according to all the time you've billed people for, you're at least 502." '

- **Your competitors or rivals**. A prime minister or president can unite his country and improve his personal rating at home by picking a fight with a weak opponent abroad. You can unite your organisation and improve your personal standing within it by having a go at corporate or sporting rivals who are not there to defend themselves. Let's suppose ABC Ltd and XYZ Ltd are fierce competitors. This is a story you could tell to ABC:

  'A very rich man wanted to get his three sons started with businesses of their own, so he asked the eldest what he wanted. The boy said he wanted a phone company, so the man bought him British Telecom. The second son was a teenager. He said he liked burgers, so the man bought him McDonalds. The third son was younger and he loved cowboy outfits, so the man bought him XYZ.'

  Obviously the story works just as well if you're appearing before XYZ employees – provided you remember to change the punchline!

  The high profile leader of a rival is also a legitimate target. Sir Richard Branson has acquired the reputation of being an extremely keen, yet ultimately unsuccessful balloonist. When he came down to earth with a bang yet again, the following one-liner did the rounds: 'Well what do you expect when you put a prick in a balloon?' Today this joke would be ideal for an audience of BA workers, but it would go down like a lead balloon with people at Virgin Atlantic (well they wouldn't laugh out loud anyway).

Most people will enjoy being the butt of your jokes – but some won't. It is worth thinking twice – and then a third time – before targeting: *your superiors, your subordinates, the audience generally.*

Don't say anything in public to embarrass or undermine your bosses. They will not be amused and you may soon discover that UB40 is not just an old pop group. Similarly don't make jokes about junior staff. If you do, you'll come across as being a nasty, vindictive bully.

If you have any doubts about anyone's likely reaction to a few well chosen little jibes, ask them whether they would mind a little mickey taking.

And don't bite the hands that clap you. A group of plumbers won't consistently laugh at jokes based on the premise that plumbers are silly. Play it safe: give them what they want – jokes about their silly suppliers and customers.

 SUGARING YOUR TEASING REMARKS WITH PRAISE

Never overlook the five elements of an after dinner speech which are almost impossible to overdo: the welcome, congratulations, flattery, thanks, praise.

A speech that is all humour – however good the humour – can sometimes become tiresome and vacuous. You need some *congratulatory and optimistic words* to counterbalance your jokes and teasing roast lines. Your speech needs to be underpinned by some good, old-fashioned sincerity. So *welcome* your fellow guests, *congratulate* any previous speakers, *flatter* the top table, *thank* the catering staff and *praise* . . . well praise just about everyone and everything.

If it moves, praise it; if it doesn't move, praise it. Praise the hosts ('the nicest of people'), the room ('these magnificent surroundings'), the occasion ('this wonderful event') and the meal ('it was nice to see the menu was in French . . . it made such a pleasant surprise each time the food arrived').

The problem is many of us are not very comfortable using gushing, extravagant language when praising individuals. Fortunately then, it's good to know that even effusive praise need not sound sycophantic in a speech.

The same flattery that could appear too florid or subservient when spoken in private seems quite acceptable in a public tribute.

Funnily enough, a sincere compliment and a teasing jibe often fit well together, each reinforcing the other in a kind of verbal synergy. The trick is first to set up a situation which you can exploit with a teasing remark, before turning this into a genuine little compliment. If the praise comes immediately after the crowd has had a good laugh at your victim's expense, its effect will be at least doubled:

> 'When I asked (*victim*) about the wedding arrangements (*set-up*), he said, "Oh, I'll leave all that to you. But I do want Bells – and at least three cases of it" (*tease*). Well I don't know about Bells, but I work with (*victim*) at Grange Hill Comprehensive . . . and I can tell you that he is certainly one of the best Teachers I know (*praise*).'

Alternatively, you may wish to build up your victim before quickly bringing him down to earth with a bang. If so, you simply reverse your tease and praise, like this:

> '(*Victim*) is quite well off, you know (*set-up*). But he never brags about it (*praise*). In fact, you can sit in a pub with him all evening and never know he had a penny (*tease*).'

③ DEALING WITH HECKLERS

During an after dinner speech, you're most unlikely to be faced by loudmouth drunks or other nasty punters. It would be rather heavy-handed, if not churlish, for a speaker to learn professional anti-heckle lines for the purpose of silencing someone who is simply enjoying the evening.

You want to show that you possess the superior wit, but to do so it shouldn't be necessary to grind your heckler into the ground.

Here are a few lines that you could use, if the situation *really* demands them:

'Would you like to step outside and say that? Good – I'll stay in here and finish my speech.'

'You know, you should be on TV – so we could turn you off.'

'Thank you, I used to know a funny version of that joke.'

However, most interruptions during after dinner speeches are likely to be good-natured and restrained and they can often can add to the occasion. Don't have a go at anyone who makes a genuine attempt to get into the spirit of things. Thank them for their contribution:

'Can I book you for my next speech?'

One last word about answering hecklers: the wittiest sally in the world will count for naught if the heckle to which it gives rise is inaudible. An old trick of the politician is, therefore, to ask the heckler to repeat his remark. The room will then fall silent and the heckler may well fail to respond in which case you could say:

'Lost for words? I'd like to help you out. Which way did you come in?'

If he does repeat his remark it will now be heard loud and clear. More often than not the moment has passed, the timing has gone awry and the heckle will be received in stoney silence.

MAKING WHAT MATTERS WORK FOR YOU

✓ Show your audience that you don't take yourself too seriously. Decide whether a little light roasting is on the menu this evening. If it is (and *only* if it is), target a little irreverent humour at a few personalities in the room. But don't roast anyone unless it's appropriate, totally in character with the occasion and clear to all that you don't really mean a word of it! If it's a corporate do, also take the opportunity to have a go at rivals.

✓ Intermix a few genuine compliments amongst your friendly, teasing digs.

✓ Laugh along with anyone in the audience who makes a genuinely humorous contribution to the evening, but put down any nasty hecklers swiftly, effectively, yet humanely.

4 Finding the Ideal Beginning and Ending

Think of your opening and closing lines as the verbal bookends of your speech. They must be constructed well enough to support and hold together everything that comes between them.

(Barry Took)

3
things that
really matter

1 **GRABBING YOUR AUDIENCE'S ATTENTION**

2 **ENDING ON JUST THE RIGHT NOTE**

3 **BRACKETING YOUR SPEECH**

How will you *begin* your speech? Should you go in loud and wake them up, or creep up quietly and lure them in to listening? The manner of your approach depends greatly upon your personal style and the image of yourself that you wish to project.

Similarly, you have a wide choice of *endings*. You can wish the company, club or society and its members good fortune in the future, repeat your thanks, quote their motto, raise another toast, or even recite a poem.

Choose your bookends with care. *They are the most important words of your speech.* Work on them until you find the pattern of words that suits your style and has exactly the effect you are after. Then *memorise* them. *You must know precisely how you are going to open and close your speech.* There is absolutely no room for any ad-libbing here.

IS THIS YOU?

(?) ● *The only opening and closing lines I can come up with are 'Good evening, ladies and gentlemen', and 'Thank you'.* ● *I sometimes hear myself opening by apologising for even being there!* ● *I need to find an opening line that will make them laugh and make me relax.* ● *When I rehearse my speech I find myself repeatedly announcing the end, which never seems to come.* ● *I want to top-and-tail my speech to make it sound really professional.*

(1) GRABBING YOUR AUDIENCE'S ATTENTION

A tourist once stopped his car in an Irish village and asked the way to Dublin. 'If I were you,' replied the thoughtful local, 'I wouldn't start from here.' You at least have the luxury of choosing where to begin your journey.

Successful communicators often ponder, consciously and subconsciously, for days over their opening words. They know that the first three sentences of their speech set the course for success or failure: a good start points towards plain sailing, a bad one makes you sail against the wind.

> 'Ladies and gentlemen, tonight I am going to suggest three reasons why this company should be interested in closer relations with Europe . . . Ingrid Bergman, Bridget Bardot and Sophia Loren . . . The perfect argument for embracing our continental cousins, for greater and varied intercourse with our fellow Europeans . . .'

You have simultaneously introduced your theme – the need to develop stronger ties with Europe – loosened collars and set the mood. You have told them: 'Don't worry folks, there may be an important message here, but this speech is going to be fun.'

A successful opening is one that:

- creates *excitement, curiosity, positive feelings* and *impact*
- convinces the audience that you *know your subject* and that you are in *control of your material*
- demonstrates your awareness of your *audience's needs, expectations, composition* and *interests*.

Here are three of the best devices that can be used to hook an after dinner audience:

- *The question hook.*
- *The anniversary hook.*
- *The humour hook.*

Let's consider each in turn.

- **The question hook.** This is a common enough oratorical device, but one all too often neglected by after dinner speakers. The hook can take many forms. Here are three dependables:

Tonight's the night: What is different and special about tonight? What will the audience get out of it? You need to be topical, personal and relevant:

> 'What is it about this evening that makes it different from any other? Would you like to know the real reason why (*some serious event*) happened? Then buckle your seat belt. It ain't what you think . . .'

The *real* reason. Funny or serious, this is going to be interesting. You have their undivided attention.

Getting them thinking: Here you open with a question that makes everyone present ask it of themselves. They are forced to make a small private self-assessment:

'What would you do if you won the Lottery . . . Save, share or splurge?'

Such a question immediately involves the audience and makes them readier to pay attention to what follows.

Being off the wall: Your opening question appears to have no relevance whatsoever, and perhaps it hasn't:

'Where do flies go in the winter?'

Or maybe you'll tell them at the end.

- **The anniversary hook**. There's nothing like telling people what a special day it is today. You're telling them that 'Today's the day!'

  'Ladies and gentlemen, this is a truly historic day! This day, the 18th of June, will always be remembered because of three world-shattering events. Napoleon finally met his Waterloo at Waterloo in 1815, pop superstar Sir Paul McCartney had his first day on Earth in 1942, and on this day in 200X, you attended tonight's banquet and heard the finest after dinner speech of your entire lifetime! Now . . . who's going to make it?'

You can find plenty of birthdays and anniversaries listed in specialist books (*Making a Wedding Speech* in the How To Books series, for example, has no less than 732 of them). You'll also find them in most daily and Sunday newspapers.

- **The humour hook**. A humorous opening must be fresh, to the point, told as succinctly as possible and timed so the punchline will elicit a laugh. Here are some examples:

'Good ladies, evening and gentlemen . . . I *knew* I should have rehearsed this speech.'

'May I begin by thanking you for the three great human qualities – faith, hope and charity. Your applause before I speak, that's faith. Applause during my speech, that's hope. Applause after my speech, that's charity.'

'Tonight I'm appearing free of charge, and I think you'll find I'm worth every penny of it.'

'Thank you. I'm not crazy about making speeches, but I've been married for 25 years and these are the only chances I get to see if my voice still works.'

'I've been asked not to bore you with a long speech this evening . . . so I'm going to do my best to bore you with a short one.'

'I asked your chairman for a complete list of everyone present, broken down by age and sex . . . but, looking round, I can't see anyone who isn't.'

(*After a formal introduction by a toastmaster*) 'Ladies and gentlemen, did he say pray *for* the silence of Pat Smith?'

Once you've hooked your audience, make a smooth transition into your first point, and before anyone knows it they're committed to listening and the process has begun.

Your opening sentence is the second most important sentence of your speech. Yes, you've guessed it: *the most important sentence is your last.*

 ENDING ON JUST THE RIGHT NOTE

There are many ways to conclude a speech. However,

remember that every speech needs its *own* ending, tailored to its content, audience and atmosphere.

A bad ending can ruin even the best speech; a good ending can salvage even a mediocre one. Yet the majority of speakers just fade away when they get to the end of their speeches.

An after dinner speech is like a love affair. Any fool can start it but to end it requires considerable skill. Your concluding remark should be to your speech what a high note is to an aria: the crescendo that triggers applause. If you can find the ideal ending you will inject that ultimate bit of magic.

A good close to an after dinner speech should fulfil three purposes. It should:

- **Pull people together**: producing the feeling that a common experience has been shared.

- **Reinforce group identity**: reminding them that they are a part of a special group.

- **Make them feel good**: creating the image or thought you want to leave etched in your audience's mind.

A shrewdly chosen tale which combines truth with fun is a far more popular finale than a glum old proverb or a plea for people to attend next month's fete.

Your closing words should provide a delectable and memorable dessert with a delicious aftertaste. As you drive over that final hill, you say: 'Look, everyone, there's the sea!'

'And that, mesdames et messieurs, is my pièce de résistance, otherwise known as my little French virgin. Bonsoir et merci bien.'

The ending, like the opening, is too important to be left to the mercy of chance or the whim of the moment.

If you can find a great little line that would perfectly round off your talk – whether it was first uttered by Tony Blair or by Lionel Blair, by Basil Hume or by Basil Brush – make any necessary little adjustments here and there and claim it as an original. Use whatever material answers your needs. Your speech will not be reviewed by literary critics. But always remember the Eleventh Commandment: Thou shalt not be found out!

On 6 September 1901 President McKinley was assassinated. Some people might know the year, but who would know the precise date, other possibly than Mrs McKinley? And she's unlikely to be in the audience. So why not claim that *today* is the anniversary? I won't tell.

'In conclusion, ladies and gentlemen, this day marks another significant anniversary. On this day (*today's date*), back in 1901, US President William McKinley was making a speech when some fellow shot him dead. Now I'm not much of one for believing in signs and omens, but there's no point in tempting fate, so I think I'll sit down.' (*You could slump back into your seat, pretending you've been shot.*)

Here are some other classic closers that you could use, adapt or personalise:

'As I said to the woman I lost my virginity to, thanks for laughing.'

'I must go now – I've got to get back to John o'Groats – and John's a very demanding lad.'

'Before I left home this evening, my little girl said to me: "Daddy, I hope they clap you and clap you and clap you after you speak. If they don't I'll cry and cry and cry forever and ever". Ladies and gentlemen, I leave it to you – do you want to be responsible for a child being miserable for the rest of her life?'

'A final thought. Always keep your words nice and sweet . . . because you never know when you're going to have to eat them.'

'And please drive home safely. We'd all much rather talk *to* you than *about* you.'

'And please don't learn the Highway Code by accident. Try to drive so that your licence expires before you do.'

You have reached your destination in style and now for the applause.

 BRACKETING YOUR SPEECH

This is a device usually associated with seasoned pros. It is designed not only to grab an audience's attention at the *start* of a speech, but also – and at the same time – to set up a situation that can be exploited at the *end*.

The idea of bracketing is to present your speech as a satisfying whole, not just as a series of jokes and stories, however well they may have been crafted and structured.

The two brackets consist of a *set-up* at the opening of the speech and a *pay-off* at the end. The words you will end with include those planted clearly at the start. Many lyricists use the same trick, establishing a phrase at the start and repeating a variation of it to round off the last line. This is how master songsmith Sammy Cahn achieved a nice little twist in the tail of *Call Me Irresponsible*:

Set-up: Call me irresponsible, call me unreliable, throw in undependable too.

Pay-off: Call me irresponsible, yes I'm unreliable, but it's undeniably true: I'm irresponsibly mad for you.

Brackets can serve you well in a speech, like this:

Set-up: Today, I confess, I've been daydreaming – both reminiscing about the past and predicting the future. We're celebrating a birthday, an anniversary. This society was founded exactly 20 years ago.

Pay-off: At the end of my reminiscing, I've come to these conclusions. We have done much for this society . . . and this society has done much for us. Each and every one of us has good reason to be proud . . . and grateful. Let's congratulate ourselves and then move on to the next 20 years.

Notice how the repetition of the words *reminiscing, society* and *20 years* helps the open-and-closed nature of the brackets and provides a pleasing symmetry. Do not simply repeat your opening. You *must* give your second bracket some memorable, amusing or thoughtful twist. Merely putting your audience back to where they started will give them the impression that you have wasted their time.

MAKING WHAT MATTERS WORK FOR YOU

√   Your opening is an opportunity. Grasp it. Devise a strong opening that's spot on for *this speech, this audience and you*. If the shoe doesn't fit, don't wear it. There are plenty of shoes that *do* fit.

√   You must end on a high note: humorous, thought-provoking, inspiring. Plan it well and practise it. The final sentence must come out perfectly. It is the last impression you leave with your audience.

√   A speech can be made truly memorable by planting a bracket at the beginning and a matching one at the end.

5 Putting it All Together

To write an after dinner speech requires
excitement, empathy, warmth, enthusiasm . . .
and flair. Flair is the sizzle in the sausage.
(Sir Peter Ustinov)

5

things that
really matter

1 **STRUCTURING YOUR MATERIAL**

2 **USING WORDS TO BE SAID, NOT READ**

3 **ADDING A SPARKLE TO YOUR SPEECH**

4 **REMEMBERING RHYTHM**

5 **PREPARING YOUR SCRIPT**

Every communication is an opportunity to throw a bridge across a void. If you do this, your speeches will have more effect than you could ever have believed possible.

Having something amusing and worthwhile to say is *never* enough. You need to know how to *use words and images to reach your audience's minds and touch their hearts.* Your speech needs flair. Flair is partly intuition – which comes from experience, imagination and a willingness to think – and a careful study of this chapter!

Today people's expectations are high and their attention spans are low. Merely to gain and hold an audience's attention requires flair. If you want to keep them interested, your speech must sparkle. So let's get polishing.

IS THIS YOU?

- *I want my speech to be more than just an unconnected series of jokes and reminiscences.*
- *The last time I made an after dinner speech I think I must have sounded as if I was reading the news. I was far too matter of fact.* • *Of course I want what I say to be entertaining, but I also want what I say to sound good.*
- *I don't know what sort of script to prepare – if any.*
- *I want to make my speech memorable . . . and for the right reasons!*

(1) STRUCTURING YOUR MATERIAL

By now, you may have collected or devised a score or more jokes, quotes, stories and friendly jibes which are, of course, all highly entertaining and in keeping with the tone and theme of your address. However, your collection is not yet a speech. It's like building a house, and you've just had the bricks delivered.

Now you have to arrange your material in a logical order so it will glide smoothly, like a narrative. This is known as *structuring*, or *routining*. There's little more tedious for an audience than having to sit through a collection of disconnected jokes and stories. In a well structured speech everything flows effortlessly to a natural conclusion – to a high point – as each joke and anecdote draws the audience in and pulls them along.

Have you noticed how entertainers, politicians and TV presenters move easily and unobtrusively from one topic to another? Like them, you can make your speech flow smoothly and elegantly from beginning to end.

Good structuring also *improves your lines*, allows you to be more *concise*, and creates a kind of *comedy synergy*. Each joke is not only complete unto itself; it develops naturally from a previous thought and serves as a set-up for the material that follows. The entertainment value of the entire speech becomes greater than the sum of the entertainment value of its component parts.

There are no hard and fast rules to assembling a script. It often comes down to a gut feeling. Humour is so subjective that in a group of half a dozen jokes, few people will agree which is the biggie you should build up to. However, the mechanics of structuring are fairly simple, involving these three stages:

- **Determine the logical progression of subtopics**.
  Sometimes this is predetermined. If your theme is your rugby club's recent tour of Scotland, you probably won't talk about the end-of-tour booze up until you've discussed some of the highlights on the field. At other times, though, there will be no obvious sequence; then the choice is at your discretion.

- **Determine the logical order of material within each subtopic**. Use a separate card for each joke and story. You can play around with your cards until that Condor moment when you hit just the order that satisfies you. Then staple or glue them together in readiness for some minor re-writing.

- **Re-write your material so it flows**. It's far easier to turn bad material into good material, or good material into great material, than it is to get everything (or even *anything*) right on the first try. After you've arranged your material in logical progression and read it through again, you'll find the individual jokes and stories just don't fit together properly. Each was written as a separate entity; now they need to be re-written to create at least the illusion of a flowing narrative.

The way a speaker keeps things flowing takes a little thought, but it's so worthwhile in its effect. How often have you winced at a clumsy transition or a hoary cliché: 'Which reminds me of the story of . . .'

You may have too many similar gags close to each other. The wording of some jokes may be too repetitive. A story may no longer need to be set up because a previous line now provides the necessary context. All these problems and others can be taken care of with some minor adjustments.

For example, suppose you have written these three jokes about your family's proud military tradition:

'My great-great grandfather fell at Waterloo . . . someone pushed him off platform nine.'

'My grandpa had a very proud service career, in the Army. He fought with Mountbatten in Burma, with Alexander in Tunis, with Monty at Alamein . . . he couldn't get on with anyone.'

'My grandpa wore Her Majesty's uniform at the Crimea. Victoria was not amused though. Said it fitted her much better.'

Obviously the set-ups are too similar for jokes so close together and the routine doesn't flow. One solution would be to change the order, change your 'great-great grandfather' into 'an ancestor' and claim you wore Her Majesty's uniform. Here's a possible re-write:

'My grandpa had a very proud service career, in the

Army. Oh yes, he fought with Mountbatten in Burma,
with Alexander in Tunis, with Monty at Alamein . . . he
couldn't get on with anyone . . . But I've been in the
Army myself, you know. Did my National Service. For two
years I wore Her majesty's uniform . . . 'course, it fitted her
better . . . But I come from an old military family – one of
my ancestors fell at Waterloo . . . some bugger pushed
him off platform nine.'

There should be three good laughs here, each progressively
louder and more sustained.

 USING WORDS TO BE SAID, NOT READ

Most people can write something to be *read*; few can write
something to be *said*. Indeed, most people are unaware that
there is even a difference.

We are used to writing things to be read: by our friends,
our relatives, our bosses, our subordinates. Such everyday
written communication is known as *text*. What we are not
used to doing is speaking our written words out loud.
Writing intended to be spoken and heard is known as
script.

Every effective speaker must recognise that there are very
important differences between text and script, namely:

Text	Script
● is a journey at the reader's pace	● is a journey at the speaker's pace
● can be re-read, if necessary	● is heard once, and only once
● can be read in any order.	● is heard in the order it is spoken.

Therefore, you must prepare a speech for an audience which *cannot* listen at its own pace; which *cannot* ask you to repeat parts it did not hear or understand; and which *cannot* choose the order in which to consider your words.

When we speak, subconsciously we choose the most appropriate words, in the best order to get our message across; but when we write script, we seem to lose the knack.

The lesson is clear: speak your words out loud before you commit them to paper. You will find that each element, each phrase, each sentence, will be built from what has gone before. Instinctively, you will take your listeners from the known to the unknown; from the general to the particular; from the present to the future.

 ADDING A SPARKLE TO YOUR SPEECH

Use words and images creatively and imaginatively and your speech will come to life. Things happen in the minds and hearts of your audience. If you look into their eyes, you can see it happen. It's a great experience.

● **Use warm words**. Words are powerful. They conjure *images*, evoke *emotions* and trigger *responses* deep within us so we *react*, often without knowing why. So-called *warm words* make us feel secure and comfortable, while *cold words* leave us uneasy and unsure. Writer Henry James said the two most beautiful words in the English language are 'summer afternoon', because they evoke just the right emotions.

In speechmaking, we work backwards from Newton's Law that every action has an equal and opposite reaction. We decide the reaction we want and work back to the words that will produce them.

In the early days of instant coffee, advertisers got off to a bad start by stressing words like *quick*, *time-saving* and *efficient*. These are all words without warmth and feeling. Makers of fresh coffee fought back with warm, happy, appetising words like *aroma*, *fresh* and *tasty*. Makers of instant coffee soon learned the lesson and their product became *delicious*, *rich* and *satisfying*. Sales *blossomed*. The rest, as they say, is history.

Once you get into the habit of looking at the emotional colouring of words, as well as their meanings, you will find yourself using the kind of language that puts listeners at ease and encourages them to react more favourably to your speeches and to you.

- **Paint word pictures**. Watching a story unfold before your eyes is dramatic and memorable. The characters move. The scenes are in colour. The whole thing has life. Merely listening to a wordy description, however enthusiastically delivered, is a yawn.

  Today most people are used to *watching* TV, not *listening* to radio. You need to give your jokes and stories a visual aspect. Let them 'see' the scenes you are describing. This means avoiding vague reference to *food* and replacing them with *pizzas* and *kebabs*. Use adjectives that conjure up specific images and trigger the senses: a *spicy* curry, a *fruity* jelly, a *savoury* pudding. Don't just tell a gag, paint it:

  'Let me tell you something about (*local character*). Soon after we met, he invited me to this thirtieth (*or whatever*) birthday party and he gave me details of his address and how to get there. He said, "A number 8 bus will bring you right to my door – 69 Della Street. Walk up to the front door and press the doorbell with your elbow." "Why my elbow?" I asked. "Because you'll have the wine in one hand and my prezzie in the other, won't you?" '

One mental word picture is worth a thousand words.

- **Engage all the senses**. Sensory details bring breadth and depth to your description. We can learn a lot from writers of popular fiction. This is how Stephen King brought a character to life in *Carrie*:

  'Norma led them around the dance floor to their table. She exuded odours of Avon soap, Woolworth's perfume and Juicy Fruit gum.'

And how about this from Katherine Mansfield:

  'Alexander and his friend in a train. Spring . . . wet lilac . . . spouting rain.'

So few words yet the wetness is palpable.

*As you speak, try to involve your audience. Allow them to do far more than just listen to you. Help them to **hear**, to **see**, to **smell**, to **touch**, to **taste**. Allow them to **experience** your speech.*

 REMEMBERING RHYTHM

A good speech should attract and hold an audience as a magnet attracts and holds iron filings. Here are a few techniques that can add an almost magical, melodic quality to your speech:

- **The rule of three**: Three is a magic number. People love to hear speakers talk to the beat of three. The effect of three words, three phrases or three sentences is powerful and memorable:

  'Things have changed a lot over the last 50 years: from the Home Guard to home computers, from Vera Lynn to

Vera Duckworth, from ration cards to scratchcards.'

- **Parallel sentences**. Sentences that are parallel add a rhythmic beauty that helps an audience anticipate and follow equal ideas:

  'To change is normal. Nothing is constant except change. Our interest rates change . . . Our clothes change . . . Our cars change . . . The face of our workforce changes . . . Our politics change . . . Our philosophies change . . . Even our cultures change. Change has become the status quo. Change is the only thing that's the same. That's normal.'

- **Alliteration**. The repetition of sounds and syllables, usually at the beginning of words, can help create just the right mood. Your speech will become special and spellbinding:

  'A generation ago, we feared typhoid more than terrorists . . . cholera more than crack . . . and rickets more than redundancy.'

Using words colourfully and creatively will bring your speech to life like a shot of whisky in a cup of coffee.

 PREPARING YOUR SCRIPT

The best talkers are those who are most natural. They are easy, fluent, friendly and amusing. No script for them. How could there be? They are talking only to us and basing what they say on our reactions as they go along. For most of us, however, that sort of performance is an aspiration rather than a description. Our tongues are not so honeyed and our words are less winged. We need a script.

But what sort of script? Cards? Notes? Speech written out in full? It's up to you. There is *no right* way of doing it. Think carefully about what kind of script suits you best and evolve a personal style. Its very familiarity will, in time, become part of its usefulness.

Here is a simple approach favoured by many speakers:

- **Write** the speech out *in full*.

- **Memorise** the opening and closing lines and *familiarise* yourself with the remainder of the speech.

- **Summarise** the speech *on one card* or *one sheet of paper* using *key words* to remind you of your sequence of jokes, anecdotes, quotations and so on.

MAKING WHAT MATTERS WORK FOR YOU

✓ Make sure your speech flows smoothly and gracefully from beginning to end, thereby creating a natural progression of ideas.

✓ Think like a listener and write like a talker. Speak your words out loud before you commit them to paper. Use effective language, not necessarily correct language.

✓ Use words and images creatively and inventively so they reach your audience's minds and touch their hearts.

✓ It is important that what you say *sounds* good. Your speech should have its own rhythm. Give it light and shade, valleys and peaks. People need valleys before they can see peaks.

✓ Rehearse using a variety of types of script – cards, notes, speech written out in full – before deciding which one suits you best.

6 Getting the Delivery Right

All communication should be personal, one-to-one. It may be 'multi-personal' – it should never be 'mass'. Talk to your audience just as you would to John and Jane Smith. What is the audience, after all, but a collection of John and Jane Smiths?
(Michael Parkinson)

4

things that
really matter

1 **FINDING YOUR STYLE**

2 **GIVING OUT THE RIGHT NON-VERBAL MESSAGES**

3 **ACTING OUT JOKES**

4 **MAKING FEAR YOUR FRIEND**

What you say is so much more important than how you say it. A speaker without a powerful or melodious voice can register just as convincingly as a great orator as soon as the audience tunes into the fun and caring behind his words.

True, a little judicious advice on delivery technique and positive body language can help smooth the edges without stifling individuality. Yet a great deal of so-called expert advice will remove the wonderfully imperfect distinctions about us and create unremarkable clones.

Essentially, you just need to identify and eliminate any negative silent messages you may be conveying to the audience through your stance and posture, your movement and gestures, and your eye contact and facial expression – and then relax and be yourself – but *yourself made large.* If you offer your homage, your humour and your heart to listeners, they cannot resist.

IS THIS YOU?

- *I want my speech to be funny, but I can't tell jokes.* ● *The last time I made a speech it felt like I was standing aside from myself, listening to a voice that didn't belong to me. It was very strange.* ● *As I stand up in front of an audience a kind of lead veil comes over me and all I can see is a close-up of myself. I hear my voice in a very loud way and every word I utter sounds awful.* ● *When I speak in public, my voice dries up and it destroys all the natural flow, all the rhythms and any kind of creative spark or anecdote that might come in is destroyed. Terrible.* ● *I am extremely nervous about giving this speech.*

① FINDING YOUR STYLE

It is exceedingly difficult to discuss style and technique in general terms, since the ability to be entertaining and to tell jokes and stories is such a personal business. However, there are certain 'rules' and guidelines which appear to be universal. Here they are:

- **Make the speech 'yours'**. Did Elvis, Sinatra and Johnny Rotten all sound the same singing *My Way*? Of course not. The artist makes the crucial difference. So, too, does the speaker.

Have you any funny faces, impersonations or mannerisms of speech which infallibly convulse friends and relatives at parties? These eccentricities, suitably broadened out, might work just as well at the dinner.

Whilst you should be aware of the importance of projecting positive body language, whatever individual characteristics you have that are special to you should be nurtured and cultivated and worked on, for it is those personal and unique quirks of appearance, personality and expression that will mark you out as a speaker with something different to offer. And that is never a bad thing.

Don't pretend to be Esther, Parky or even Jerry. Be yourself.

- **Be conversational.** Sitting leisurely, with family, friends or colleagues, your conversation will be naturally relaxed and chatty, because that is the language of easy communication. Casual conversation is not constructed in a literary way. You do not always finish your sentences. You repeat yourself. You use ungrammatical constructions but you are obeying a different set of rules. You are obeying the rules of effective spoken communication which have been learnt, instinctively, down the ages. Don't abandon these rules when you speak in public.

  If you 'put on an act' you will be perceived as phoney, boring, or lacking in personality. As a result, you won't come over well. Certainly you may need to speak a little louder or make other concessions to accommodate the needs of your audience but, in essence, nothing in your delivery style should change.

The key is to recognise what you are doing when you 'get it right' and achieve any successful communication, be it formal or informal, business or social, and then stay with it in any given situation, regardless of the stress level.

- **Use emotion to good effect.** C.S. Forrester reminds us that 'Words spoken from the heart carry more weight than all the artifices of rhetoric.' You should feel free to display strong personal feelings when you speak. However, you *must* be genuine. False heartiness, cheap sincerity and – worst of all – crocodile tears will all be obvious to an audience.

- **Be heard**. You must be audible. If you are not, all else is lost. If there is public address equipment available, find out how it works, get plenty of practice and then use it. Don't trust in luck and don't believe people who tell you to leave it all to them. Accept personal responsibility. You are the one who will look awkward if things go wrong.

If there is no sound-enhancing equipment, speak as clearly and as loudly as is necessary to be heard. If the only other person in the room was at the back, you would talk to him or her naturally, at the right level, without shouting or strain, by:

- keeping your head up
- opening your mouth wider than during normal speech
- using clearer consonants
- slowing down.

If you remember that you must be heard by that same person, at the back, during your speech, however many other people may be in the room, you will make those same four *natural* adjustments to your delivery.

 ## GIVING OUT THE RIGHT NON-VERBAL MESSAGES

We *speak* with our vocal cords but we *communicate* with our whole body. An audience does a lot more than listen to a speech – *it experiences it*. Everything about a speaker's manner and demeanour contributes to the overall impression that the audience takes away.

Too many speakers seem to think they can only be seen when they stand and deliver. This isn't the case. If you slurp your soup, spill peas all over the floor and ignore your neighbours' valiant attempts at making polite conversation, the audience will notice. It's no good becoming good Dr Jekyll when you stand up; your audience will have already seen nasty Mr Hyde.

Body language is potent. When you address a group of people they are constantly responding consciously and unconsciously to what your body is saying to them.

So what hidden messages do you give out before, during and after your speech? If you are unsure, watch yourself in a mirror, or ask a kind but critical friend. You may find that you need to work on one or more of the following:

- stance and posture

- movement and gestures

- eye contact and facial expression.

However, remember that while each of these may be considered in isolation, a positive change made to any of them will also have a direct and immediate positive effect on the others.

- **Stance and posture**. These are important. You are making a fundamental statement with your body. An aligned, upright posture conveys a message of confidence and integrity.

Early man frightened his enemies by inflating his chest and spreading his arms to present a much wider profile (see Figure 1). Modern man uses exactly the same technique, consciously or unconsciously, when he wants to convince others of his dominance (see Figure 2).

Fig. 1. The aggressive caveman

This domineering stance is
unsuitable for making an after
dinner speech

A friendly, upright, open,
unthreatening stance is far
preferable

Fig. 2. Don't threaten the audience!

Our instincts tell us that people who shield themselves –
even with just their arms – are defensive (see Figure 3);
while people who do not shield themselves are perceived as
open and friendly (see Figure 4).

- **Movement and gestures.** You should be far more than
  just a talking head. You don't want to be so motionless
  that you look like a statue on loan from Madame
  Tussaud's, but equally you shouldn't attempt an
  impersonation of racing pundit John McCririck's arm-
  waving histrionics.

Fig. 3. The defensive cavewoman

Crossed arms are seen as defensive and negative

Open arms and open palms are considered friendly and positive

Fig. 4. Don't defend yourself against the audience!

Early man attacked his victims by holding a weapon above their heads and bringing it down with great force (see Figure 5). Our legacy from this is that, even today, our ancestral memories perceive similar positions and movements as hostile (see Figure 6).

- **Eye contact and facial expression**. These are crucial aspects of effective communication because they gain and then maintain an audience's attention, create rapport, and give you valuable feedback as to how well you are coming over.

Fig. 5. The hostile caveman

Hands and fingers pointing
upwards and finger-wagging
sweeping movements are
seen as threatening

Open palms with fingers
downward are seen as
unthreatening and
friendly

Fig. 6. Don't be hostile to the audience!

*The worst you can do, apart from mumbling inaudibly, is not to look
at your audience.*

You should have memorised your opening and closing lines,
so *look* at your audience as you deliver them. During the
middle of your speech, try to keep your head up from your
script for most of the time.

It is in the nature of after dinner speaking that you will
find the quickest response from the front of the audience.

But don't ignore the poor folks at the back who will feel more and more alienated if you appear to be having a private party with your mates down at the front. Give everyone the benefit of your big blue eyes and flashing smile once in a while.

The effectiveness of your speech will depend, to a large extent, on your body language. A confident stance, accompanied by relevant gestures and lively facial expressions, will capture your audience's attention and greatly enhance the impact of your speech.

 ACTING OUT JOKES

There are fundamental differences in written, spoken and visual humour. To illustrate this let's consider how a story can improve in the *telling* and *showing* over the bald facts on the printed page. Here is a silly story you could relate – together with some suggested 'stage directions' for acting it out:

> 'My landlady. Funny woman. (*Put your forefinger to your temple to indicate that she's not all there.*) One day she met me in the hall when I was on my own – Jane was putting manure on the rhubarb – I prefer custard. Anyway, the landlady said, "Would you like to come into my parlour and see my pussy?" Her *cat*. So I said, "Love to" – anything for a laugh. So she said, "Come in", and we went into her parlour. And there, on the mat, in front of the fire, sat – the cat. (*indicate that he is to your left.*) She said, "This is Clinton." "Oh yes?" I said, "he's very nice." She said, "Yes, he comes from China – He's a Peking Tom. And he's clever too. He can play the piano." I said, "Can he? The cat? Clinton?" She said, "Yes – would you like to see?" I said, "You bet." So she said (*turn slightly to your left*),

"Clinton," (*turn to the front*) that's the cat . . . sitting on the mat . . . she said (*turn slightly to your left*), "Clinton, play." (*Turn to front.*) And Clinton got up – the cat – walked across the room, jumped on the piano stool, sat down on a pile of cushions. (*Let your fingers do the walking from your left to your right side and then indicate how he jumps up onto the stool.*) And he began to play. The cat. Clinton. Fantastic – arpeggios, scales, runs up and down the keyboard. (*Play an imaginary piano with gusto.*) I said, "My goodness me, he does play well." She said, "He does, doesn't he?" I said, "That's clever. And that piece of music he's playing: that's very nice. I've never heard it before – did he write it himself?" She said, "Yes, he did." I said, "It's marvellous. Have you thought about having it orchestrated?" Well, you've never seen a cat move so fast in all your life.' (*Use your fingers to indicate the cat's speedy exit.*)

The precise wording and style of delivery of a joke or story, of course, is *yours*, not mine. but I hope this simple example will encourage you to look at your material a little more carefully to see what can be extracted over and above the obvious punchline reaction.

 MAKING FEAR YOUR FRIEND

Fear is nothing to be frightened of. People get nervous because they are afraid of failing, of looking foolish, and not living up to expectations. Nervousness is caused by the fear of looking ridiculous to others.

Few speakers claim to be able to speak without any nerves. Some will say that lack of nerves is not only unlikely, it is undesirable. They need the adrenaline to carry them along. So how do you make things easier for yourself? Be assured that excessive worry *is* avoidable, if you follow this advice:

- **Rehearse.** Why do some actors freeze or fumble on the opening night and then pick up a British Theatre Drama Award six months later? It's a fear of unfamiliarity. As the days, weeks and months go by, the fear abates and the quality of the performance improves.

The more rehearsal, the more the certainty of success and greater peace of mind.

Words become more familiar. Awkward juxtapositions are smoothed out. You suddenly think of a way of saying a stuffy sentence in a more straightforward and colloquial style. At the same time you will recognise the parts of your speech that hit the spot, the parts that require a little fine tuning, and the parts that are simply not worth including.

- **Have the right attitude.** Tell yourself that you are going to make a great little speech. And *believe* it. The largely untapped power of positive thinking really is enormous. It has been estimated that 85% of performance is directly related to attitude. Unfortunately, many speakers think they are going to fail and, with this attitude, this becomes a self-fulfilling prophecy.

- **Visualise success.** Visualisation is the planting of mental images into the subconscious mind. These images must be vivid and real – you must be able to *see*, to *hear*, to *touch*, to *taste* and to truly *live* them.

If you can vividly imagine an event happening, it will greatly strengthen the likelihood of it actually happening.

So reinforce your positive attitude with a positive visualisation of your speech. Imagine yourself talking in a relaxed and confident manner. You are looking good. They love your opening hook. But it gets better; your stories and jokes wow them. They are eating out of your hand. Then comes that big finish. Nobody could have topped that. Listen to their cheers and applause. Now that's what I call an after dinner speech! What you used to call fear can now be re-named excitement and anticipation.

MAKING WHAT MATTERS WORK FOR YOU

✓ The challenge is to give out the right silent messages to your audience and to project your personality, not suppress it. Knowing that you not only can, but also should be yourself will stop you worrying about your 'performance', and allow you to concentrate on what really matters: being enthusiastic and being entertaining.

✓ Use your well-rehearsed opening to create a positive response from the audience. This will help you relax and this will manifest itself in positive body language. You will have broken into a wonderful virtuous circle. Positive body language not only reflects positive feelings, it creates them.

✓ Be more than just a talking head. Act your jokes out.

✓ The greatest antidotes to nerves are preparation and attitude. Whether you think you will succeed or whether you think you will fail, you will probably be right.